STARTERS

Homes

Rosie McCormick

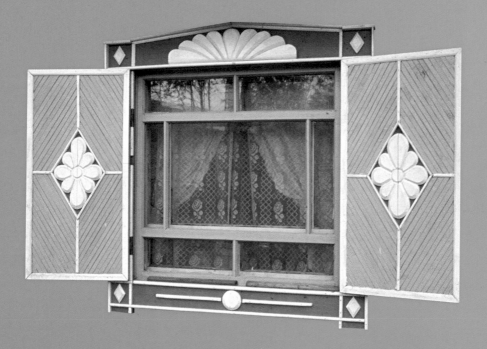

Text copyright © Rosie McCormick 2003

Consultant: John Lace
Language consultant: Andrew Burrell
Design: Perry Tate Design

Published in Great Britain in 2003
by Wayland, an imprint of
Hachette Children's Books, an Hachette UK Company, www.hachette.co.uk
This paperback edition published in 2005

Reprinted in 2006, 2008 (twice) and 2009 by Wayland, an imprint of Hachette
Children's Books

The publishers would like to thank the following for allowing us to reproduce their
pictures in this book: Robert Harding; 5 (top) / Impact; cover, 6, 9, 15, 21-22 / Corbis;
5 (bottom), title page, 7, 10, 13-14, 16-17, 20, 24 (fourth from top) / Britstock; 8 /
Eye Ubiquitous; 11 (bottom), 12, 19 (top), 24 (top and bottom) / Still Pictures; 4, 11
(top), 24 (third from top) / James Davis Travel Photography; 18, 19 (bottom), 24
(second from top) / Science Photo Library; 23

A Catalogue record for this book is available from the British Library.

ISBN: 978 0 7502 4426 8

Printed and bound in China

Hachette Children's Books
338 Euston Road, London NW1 3BH

Contents

What is a home?

The place where we live, eat, sleep and play is called our home. There are many different kinds of homes.

Sometimes natural materials such as wood, stone or mud are used to build homes. Man-made materials such as bricks, concrete or glass are used too.

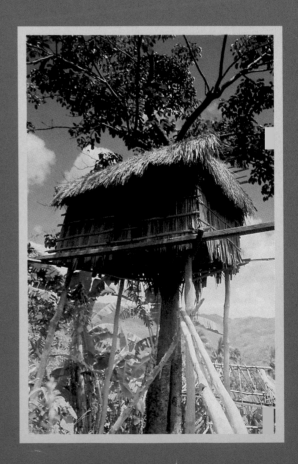

Tree houses keep people safe from dangerous animals.

Igloos are made of frozen snow.

Cottages are built to last a very long time.

Homes made out of wood

In many parts of the world, wood is used to build homes. Wood is a strong material and it is easy to build with. Wooden houses help keep the heat inside.

In Northern Europe, many wooden houses have sloping roofs so winter snow can slide off.

In Russia, wooden summerhouses are beautifully decorated.

In the Dominican Republic, people paint their wooden houses in bright colours.

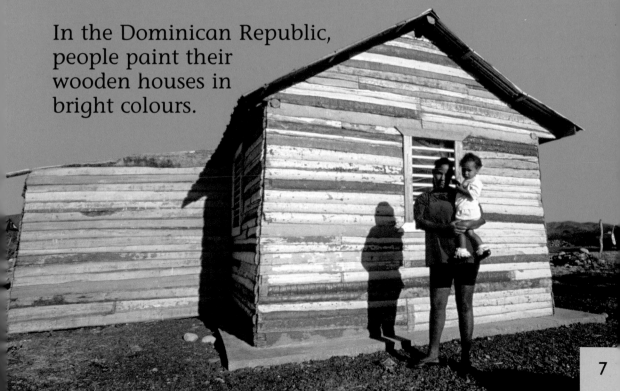

Homes made out of mud

In hot, dry countries people make mud bricks. The sun bakes the mud hard. Sun-dried bricks can last for hundreds of years.

Mud is found locally so there is plenty to use.

8

In Rwanda, Africa, people live in round houses made of poles, twigs and mud.

The thick mud brick walls help to keep the house cool.

People who live in countries where there is a lot of water, such as Indonesia and Malaysia, live in houses on stilts.

Stilt homes keep water, snakes and other creatures out.

Some people live
in homes made
out of huge leaves
found nearby.

These homes sit on giant
reed mats that can float!

Rocks and caves

For thousands of years people have made homes in caves and rocky places. Caves provide good shelter from the hot sun and cold winds.

In Spain, some people have made homes out of caves in hills.

In the Australian desert, it's so hot that some people live in underground homes called Dugouts.

These large rock towers in Turkey have been turned into homes.

Mobile homes

Some mobile homes, like caravans and boats, carry people about. Others, like tents, are carried by people.

In Mongolia, people have to move their animals to fresh land. So they move their homes too.

Sometimes people live in boats.

In Asia, lots of people live in houseboats. They cook, eat, sleep and even work on the boats.

Unusual homes

Sometimes people build houses that look a little strange! Would you like to live in one of these houses?

This houseboat in North America is very unusual!

The walls of this house in New Mexico are made out of old tyres.

This house is made out of mud and tin cans.

Glass, brick and steel

Today many people live in homes made out of brick, concrete, glass and steel. In big cities, people often live in homes built on top of each other. These are called apartments.

In Europe, North America and Australia most people live in homes built for one family.

Long ago, kings and queens built grand castles made of brick and stone to live in.

Homeless

People who are homeless have nowhere to live. There are millions of homeless people in the world today.

Many homeless people are refugees. Often, refugees do not have homes because of earthquakes, floods and war.

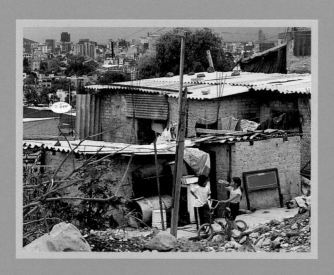

Homeless people
are often poor
and cannot afford
a proper home.

Some homeless people live
in cardboard boxes
on the streets.

Communities

Most people are part of a community that they also call home. A community is made up of people living and working together. Villages, towns and cities are communities.

People work together to keep their communities safe, clean and happy.

Although people live in different places
and in different ways, one thing is certain,
Planet Earth is our home.
We must all take
good care of
this special
home.

Glossary and index